Language Builders

Phillip and Penny Learn about
PRONOUNS

by Joanna Jarc Robinson
illustrated by Caroline Hu

Content Consultant
Roxanne Owens
Associate Professor, Elementary Reading
DePaul University

NORWOOD HOUSE PRESS
CHICAGO, ILLINOIS

Norwood House Press
P.O. Box 316598
Chicago, Illinois 60631
For information regarding Norwood House Press, please visit
our website at:
www.norwoodhousepress.com or call 866-565-2900.

Editor: Melissa York
Designer: Jake Nordby
Project Management: Red Line Editorial

Paperback ISBN: 978-1-60357-705-2

The Library of Congress has cataloged the original hardcover
edition with the following call number: 2014030275

Manufactured in the United States of America in North
Mankato, Minnesota.
262N—122014

Words in **black bold** are defined in the glossary.

Pets and Pronouns

I am so excited! My sister, Penny, and I earned good grades on our report cards, so Mom told us we could each get a pet! I want a boy hamster and Penny wants a girl hamster.

Mom said she would take us to the pet store on Saturday. We can pick out our hamsters and buy all the supplies for them.

Mom also said I have homework to do this weekend. I was sick and missed two days of school this week. My class was learning about **pronouns**. Maybe Penny will help me since she learned about pronouns last year. I hope I finish it quickly so I can play with my new pet.

I cannot wait! I must think of the perfect name for him. Hmm . . .

By Phillip, age 8

"Lucinda? No. Marley? No. Anastasia? No. Naming a hamster is difficult!" said Penny between bites of breakfast.

Phillip was trying to think of names, too. "I'm thinking something powerful, like Thor or Zeus."

"How about Captain Furrypants?" suggested Phillip and Penny's dad, Mr. Lee, as he set more pancakes on the table. Phillip laughed so hard orange juice almost shot out of his nose.

"There is something else we should discuss before we go to the pet store," Mrs. Lee said. "You missed some school last week when you were sick. You still have to complete your pronoun homework."

Phillip looked at his homework sheet again. Mrs. Lee said, "It might be a good idea to take it with us. I bet you will hear lots of pronouns at the pet shop."

Directions: Listen for these pronouns in everyday conversations. When you hear one, write a complete sentence using that pronoun.

he	I	we	they
she	mine	us	their
him	myself	you	this
her	it	what	those

"What is a pronoun anyway?" asked Phillip. "Is it like a noun?"

Penny had the answer. "Sort of. A noun is a person, place, or thing. Pronouns take the place of other nouns. A pronoun is another way to identify something."

"So what does that mean?" asked Phillip.

Penny offered the perfect example: "I could say, '*She* is still drinking *her* coffee so we cannot leave for the pet store yet.' *She* takes the place of *Mom* and *her* takes the place of *Mom's* coffee."

"Good example, Penny," said Mr. Lee. "We use *she* because Mom is a female. We use *he* if the subject is male. And don't forget—*we* is also a pronoun. *We* takes the place of two or more people: Mom, Dad, Penny, and Phillip."

"*We* is a **plural** pronoun," added Penny. "So are *us* and *they* and *their*. *I* and *she* and *her* are all **singular**. They refer to only one person."

"I see why using pronouns makes sense," said Phillip. "It's easier to say *we* than saying all those names, or saying Mom or Penny over and over."

"Exactly," said Mr. Lee. "A pronoun should refer back to a noun you were already talking about. Otherwise it can get confusing."

Mrs. Lee chimed in, "Maybe Penny can help you with your pronoun homework. She just learned about them last year."

"Yes, *I* can help *you*," said Penny, pointing to herself and then to her brother.

Everyone laughed. The family cleaned up the breakfast dishes and got ready to go to the pet store.

Phillip studied his homework in the car so he would know which pronoun words to listen for. Then he folded the paper and stuffed it in his pocket. When they arrived, Phillip and Penny ran inside and headed straight for the hamsters. They passed the fish, the ferrets, and cat food before they reached the big glass cage. There were so many hamsters: white ones, brown ones, white and brown ones, and orange-colored ones.

Penny said, "Which one do you want? They are so cute! I love them all!"

Phillip heard three pronouns: *you* and *they* and *I*. He pulled out his homework and jotted down three sentences.

Mrs. Lee watched him write. Then she explained, "Every pronoun is either first-person, second-person, or third-person. The person of the pronoun is what it refers to. First-person pronouns refer to the speaker—*I* or *we* or *me* or *my*."

"Second-person pronouns show who you are talking to—that's *you*," added Penny.

"And third-person pronouns are who or what you are talking about—*she*, *he*, *they*, *them*," finished Mrs. Lee.

"I want this one!" said Penny, pointing to a little brown and white hamster in the corner. "Look at those little beady eyes! These hamsters are adorable!"

Phillip heard several more pronouns as Penny spoke. He wrote sentences for *this* and *those*.

Mr. Lee jumped in. "*This*, *that*, *these*, and *those* are demonstrative pronouns. They demonstrate the distance between the speaker and the object. *This* and *that* are singular. *This* hamster is relatively close. *That* hamster is farther away," he said, pointing to the different hamsters in the cage. "*These* and *those* are plural. *These* hamsters are huddled together in the corner. *Those* hamsters are hiding under the bedding."

Just then, a sales clerk asked, "Do you need some help?"

Phillip and Penny said, "We both do!" at the same time.

"*You* is a special pronoun," said Penny. "It can be singular or plural."

"When the clerk said *you*, that was a plural pronoun," observed Phillip.

"That's right!" said Mrs. Lee. She explained to the clerk that they were going to pick out hamsters for pets.

"First, will you need one cage or two?" asked the clerk.

Mom said, "They will share one."

Phillip and Penny were not sure about sharing. Then Phillip said, "We can take turns with them. One week, you can keep them in your room. The next week, I will keep them in mine."

Penny thought that sounded reasonable. Then, she thought about pronouns again. "Did you know you just used subject pronouns and object pronouns in your sentences?"

Phillip did not realize it. Penny explained, "*We* is the subject pronoun because that is who the sentence is about. Subject pronouns are usually at the beginning of the sentence. *Them* is the object of the sentence and describes who the action is happening to. It usually comes after a **verb** or a **preposition**."

Phillip was busy trying to remember all about the different kinds of pronouns while he was choosing a hamster. He pointed to the one he wanted, a male. "He looks just right!" said Phillip.

"Can I hold him?" Phillip asked. The clerk handed the hamster to Phillip.

"See what I did there?" said Phillip to Mr. Lee. "I used pronouns in a question where *I* am the subject and *him* is the object."

"Nice work," said Mr. Lee. "You can hold him for a second, then we will put him in the box so you can take him home. It will be safer that way."

After the hamster was safe in its box, Phillip pulled out his homework and wrote several more sentences.

"*We, him, you, it,*" he said, "Pronouns are in almost every sentence I hear. I'm going to be finished in no time."

Penny pointed to the hamster she wanted. "This one is a female," the clerk said.

"That one is mine!" squealed Penny. "Oh my goodness, her fur is so soft!"

Mrs. Lee pointed out that there were several **possessive** pronouns in Penny's sentences. "A possessive pronoun shows who or what has something, or whom it belongs to," she explained.

Penny agreed. "When I said *mine*, that means she belongs to me. Then I said *her* fur is so soft—it's her fur. It belongs to her."

Phillip got it. He joked, "You also said *my* goodness—that goodness belongs to you!" They all laughed.

The family had many questions for the clerk. They asked, "What kind of food do they eat? Which water bottle is the right size? Which bedding should we get? Who makes the best hamster treats?"

Mrs. Lee said, "We just used several interrogative pronouns. Those are pronouns that ask a question, like *what, which, who*." Luckily, the clerk was able to answer all of their questions. The clerk helped the family find all the right hamster supplies.

"Enjoy your new pets," said the clerk as they left.

When they got in the car, Phillip checked his homework. He only had a couple of sentences left to write.

"We still have to think of names for our pets," said Penny. "Mom, Dad, will you help us? We cannot think of names all by ourselves."

Mr. Lee said, "Sure! But did you know you just used reflexive pronouns? It's a pronoun that refers back to the subject of the sentence. In this case, *ourselves* refers back to *we*. You said, '*We* cannot think of names all by *ourselves*.'"

Penny joked, "I guess *I* should pat *myself* on the back for using reflexive pronouns."

They got home and set up the cage in Phillip's room. "Their home looks awesome," said Penny.

"*Their*!" exclaimed Phillip, which made Penny jump. "That's the last pronoun I need!"

Which one do **you** want?
They are so cute!
I love them all!
I want **this** one.
Look at **those** little beady eyes.
He looks just right.
Can I hold **him**?
We can put him in the box.
It will be much safer that way.
That one is **mine**.
Her fur is so soft.
She belongs to me.
What kind of food do they eat?
Will you help **us**?
I should pat **myself** on the back.
Their home looks awesome.

Just then, Mom came into the room with some lunch for the kids. "Did you come up with any names yet?" she wondered.

"Nope," said Penny. "Not yet," added Phillip.

Penny took a bite of her sandwich. Suddenly, she had an idea. "I know what we could name them!"

Phillip was excited. "What? What?" he asked eagerly.

"Peanut Butter and Jelly!" shouted Penny. "Yours could be Peanut Butter and mine can be Jelly!"

Phillip smiled. He liked those names. They were perfect. Penny and Phillip ate their peanut butter and jelly sandwiches. Then they spent all day watching their new pets, Peanut Butter and Jelly.

Know Your Pronouns

Pronouns take the place of nouns in a sentence. Use pronouns instead of repeating the same noun over and over. Pronouns should refer back to a noun that was already introduced, or else they can be confusing.

Pronouns are singular if they refer to one person, place, or thing. They are plural if they refer to more than one thing. *You* can be singular or plural. Pronouns can be first-person, second-person, or third-person. First-person refers to the speaker: *I, we, me, my.* Second-person is *you*, the person being talked to. Third person is what is talked about: *she, he, they, them.* These pronouns match the gender of the subject, if it is male or female.

Subject pronouns like *he* or *we* are who the sentence is about. Object pronouns like *them* or *her* show what the action is happening to.

There are several specific types of pronouns. Demonstrative pronouns—*this, that, these,* and *those*—tell the distance between the speaker and the object. *This* is nearby, *that* is far away. A possessive pronoun like *mine* or *hers* shows whom something belongs to. Interrogative pronouns like *what* or *who* ask a question. And reflexive pronouns like *myself* or *ourselves* refer back to the subject of the sentence.

Look back at page 28. How many pronouns can you find?

Writing Activity

Imagine that you get to pick out a new pet. Write a short story about your new pet. Use complete sentences. Be sure to include pronouns. Think about these questions to help you: What kind of pet would you choose? Why would you choose that kind of pet? Describe what your pet might look like. What color is your pet's fur or skin? How big is your pet? What does your pet's eyes, nose, and mouth look like? Does it have a tail? How would you care for your pet? What would your pet eat? Where would your pet live? Where would your pet sleep? What would you name your pet?

Read back through your story. Make sure it is clear what all the pronouns refer to. Draw a picture of your pet if you like. Share your story and your picture with a friend or your family.

Glossary

plural: more than one of something.

possessive: showing ownership.

preposition: a word that describes how words in a sentence relate to each other. It may show a time or a place relationship.

pronouns: words that take the place of a noun, like a person or thing.

singular: one of something.

verb: a word that shows action (like run, jump) or being (am, have).

For More Information

Books

Fisher, Doris. *Slam Dunk Pronouns*. Pleasantville, NY: Gareth Stevens, 2008.

Lambert, Deborah. *Pronouns*. New York: Weigl, 2010.

Websites

Balloon Pronoun Game
http://www.softschools.com/language_arts/grammar/pronoun/
balloon_game/
Play this online game to practice identifying pronouns.

Pro Nounsense
http://www.mcwdn.org/grammar/pronounhome.html
At this website, read more about pronouns. Then take quizzes to test yourself.

About the Author

Joanna Jarc Robinson is a funny, quirky, creative children's author, illustrator, and education professional, specializing in Pre-K–8 educational content.